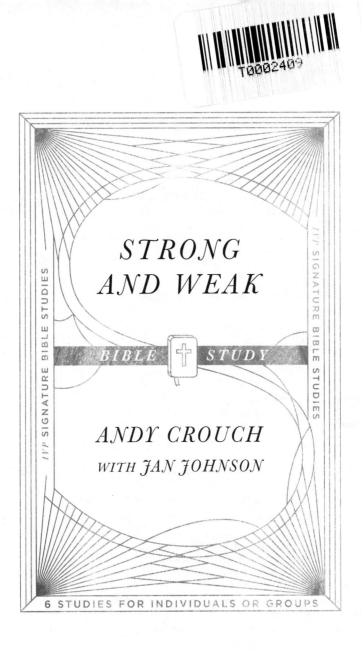

STRONG AND WEAK

BIBLE ✝ STUDY

ANDY CROUCH

WITH JAN JOHNSON

6 STUDIES FOR INDIVIDUALS OR GROUPS

IVP SIGNATURE BIBLE STUDIES

ivp

An imprint of InterVarsity Press
Downers Grove, Illinois

InterVarsity Press
P.O. Box 1400 | Downers Grove, IL 60515-1426
ivpress.com | email@ivpress.com

This study guide is based on and adapts material from *Strong and Weak*, ©2016 by Andy Crouch.

InterVarsity Press® is the publishing division of InterVarsity Christian Fellowship/USA®. For more information, visit intervarsity.org.

While any stories in this book are true, some names and identifying information may have been changed to protect the privacy of individuals.

The publisher cannot verify the accuracy or functionality of website URLs used in this book beyond the date of publication.

Cover design and image composite: David Fassett
Interior design: Daniel van Loon

ISBN 978-0-8308-4712-9 (print) | ISBN 978-0-8308-4713-6 (digital)

Printed in the United States of America ♾

Library of Congress Cataloging-in-Publication Data
A catalog record for this book is available from the Library of Congress.

29 28 27 26 25 24 23 22 | 13 12 11 10 9 8 7 6 5 4 3 2 1

CONTENTS

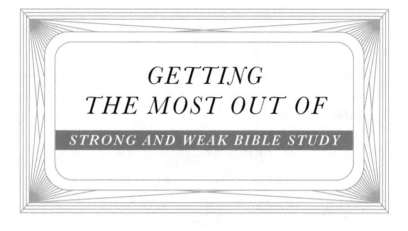

GETTING
THE MOST OUT OF
STRONG AND WEAK BIBLE STUDY

KNOWING CHRIST is where faith begins. From there we are shaped through the essentials of discipleship: Bible study, prayer, Christian community, worship, and much more. We learn to grow in Christlike character, pursue justice, and share our faith with others. We persevere through doubts and gain wisdom for daily life. These are the topics woven into the IVP Signature Bible Studies. Working through this series will help you practice the essentials by exploring biblical truths found in classic books.

HOW IT'S PUT TOGETHER

Each session includes an opening quotation and suggested reading from the book *Strong and Weak*, a session goal to help guide your study, reflection questions to stir your thoughts on the topic, the text of the Bible passage, questions for exploring the passage, response questions to help you apply what you've learned, and a closing suggestion for prayer.

The workbook format is ideal for personal study and also allows group members to prepare in advance for discussions and record discussion notes. The responses you write here can form a permanent record of your thoughts and spiritual progress.

Throughout the guide are study-note sidebars that may be useful for group leaders or individuals. These notes do not give the answers, but they do provide additional background information on certain questions and can challenge participants to think deeper or differently about the content.

WHAT KIND OF GUIDE IS THIS?

The studies are not designed to merely tell you what one person thinks. Instead, through inductive study, they will help you discover for yourself what Scripture is saying. Each study deals with a particular passage—rather than jumping around the Bible—so that you can really delve into the biblical author's meaning in that context.

The studies ask three different kinds of questions about the Bible passage:

* *Observation* questions help you to understand the content of the passage by asking about the basic facts: who, what, when, where, and how.

* *Interpretation* questions delve into the meaning of the passage.

* *Application* questions help you discover implications for growing in Christ in your own life.

These three keys unlock the treasures of the biblical writings and help you live them out.

This is a thought-provoking guide. Each question assumes a variety of answers. Many questions do not have "right" answers, particularly questions that aim at meaning or application. Instead, the questions should inspire readers to explore the passage more thoroughly.

This study guide is flexible. You can use it for individual study, but it is also great for a variety of groups—student, professional, neighborhood, or church groups. Each study takes about forty-five minutes in a group setting or thirty minutes in personal study.

SUGGESTIONS FOR INDIVIDUAL STUDY

1. This guide is based on a classic book that will enrich your spiritual life. If you have not read *Strong and Weak*, you may want to read the portion recommended in the "Read" section before you begin your study. The ideas in the book will enhance your study, but the Bible text will be the focus of each session.

2. Begin each session with prayer, asking God to speak to you from his Word about this particular topic.

3. As you read the Scripture passage, reproduced for you from the New International Version, you may wish to mark phrases that seem important. Note in the margin any questions that come to your mind.

4. Close with the suggested prayer found at the end of each session. Speak to God about insights you have gained. Tell him of any desires you have for specific growth. Ask him to help you attempt to live out the principles described in that passage. You may wish to write your own prayer in this guide or a journal.

SUGGESTIONS FOR GROUP MEMBERS

Joining a Bible study group can be a great avenue to spiritual growth. Here are a few guidelines that will help you as you participate in the studies in this guide.

1. Reading the recommended portion of *Strong and Weak*, before or after each session, will enhance your study and understanding of the themes in this guide.

2. These studies use methods of inductive Bible study, which focuses on a particular passage of Scripture and works on it in depth. So try to dive into the given text instead of referring to other Scripture passages.

3. Questions are designed to help a group discuss together a passage of Scripture in order to understand its content, meaning, and implications. Most people are either natural talkers or natural listeners, yet this type of study works best if all members participate more or less evenly. Try to curb any natural tendency toward either excessive talking or excessive quiet. You and the rest of the group will benefit!

4. Most questions in this guide allow for a variety of answers. If you disagree with someone else's comment, gently say so. Then explain your own point of view from the passage before you.

5. Be willing to lead a discussion, if asked. Much of the preparation for leading has already been accomplished in the writing of this guide.

6. Respect the privacy of people in your group. Many people share things within the context of a Bible study group that they do not want to be public knowledge. Assume that personal information spoken within the group setting is private, unless you are specifically told otherwise.

7. We recommend that all groups agree on a few basic guidelines. You may wish to adapt this list to your situation:

   a. Anything said in this group is considered confidential and will not be discussed outside the group unless specific permission is given to do so.

   b. We will provide time for each person present to talk if he or she feels comfortable doing so.

c. We will talk about ourselves and our own situations, avoiding conversation about other people.

d. We will listen attentively to each other.

e. We will pray for each other.

8. Enjoy your study. Prepare to grow!

SUGGESTIONS FOR GROUP LEADERS

There are specific suggestions to help you in the "Leading a Small Group" section. It describes how to lead a group discussion, gives helpful tips on group dynamics, and suggests ways to deal with problems that may arise during the discussion. With such helps, someone with little or no experience can lead an effective group study. Read this section carefully, even if you are leading only one group meeting.

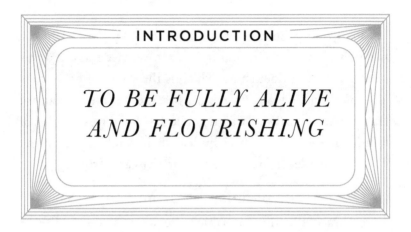

TO BE FULLY ALIVE AND FLOURISHING

WHAT ARE WE MEANT TO BE? We are meant to flourish—not just to survive, but to thrive; not just to exist, but to explore and expand. *Gloria Dei vivens homo*, the early Christian bishop Irenaeus wrote. A loose—but by no means inaccurate—translation of those words has become popular: "The glory of God is a human being fully alive."

To flourish is to be fully alive. When we read or hear those words something in us wakes up, sits up a bit straighter, leans ever so slightly forward. To be fully alive would connect us not just to our own proper human purpose but to the very heights and depths of divine glory. To live fully in these transitory lives on this fragile earth in such a way that we somehow participate in the glory of God—that would be flourishing. And that is what we are meant to do.

Why are we so far from what we're meant to be? Flourishing is a paradoxical process. Like every paradox, it requires that we embrace two things that at first seem like opposites and that don't seem to go together at all. But in fact, if you do not have both, you do not have flourishing, and you do not create it for others.

Here's the paradox: flourishing comes from being both *strong* and *weak*.

Flourishing requires us to embrace both authority and vulnerability, both capacity and frailty. Yet we have forgotten this basic paradox of flourishing, which is the secret of being fully alive. We usually fear vulnerability because it's so risky. But we fear authority too. We are afraid of both sides of this paradox of flourishing—and we especially fear their combination in the only way that leads to real life for ourselves and others.

THE DIMENSIONS OF POWER

To embrace the life for which we were made—a life of flourishing—it's important to pursue greater authority and greater vulnerability at the same time. A simple chart, the kind of thing you can draw on a napkin, provides a sketch of the paradox of flourishing.

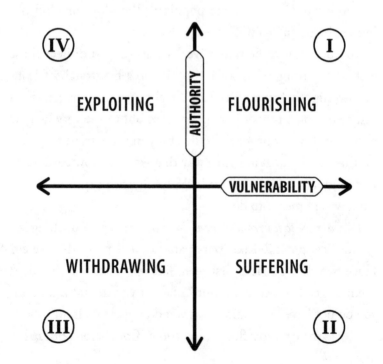

Jesus perfectly blended both authority and vulnerability in a way that empowered the weak with authority and confounded the powerful with vulnerability.

Some of us instinctively identify with, or aspire to, the vulnerability dimension. Perhaps that has been the primary reality of our lives or of the community or family into which we were born, making us keenly aware of the limits of our power and the precariousness of our circumstances. Or we may aspire to identify with vulnerable people and places. From those places and with those people, we look at Jesus and see vulnerability. Jesus identified with the vulnerable in his birth, life, and death. Whether we identify with vulnerability or aspire to it, Jesus is there.

On the other hand, some of us identify with or aspire to authority. We have been told we can make a difference in the world, and we've been given opportunities for creativity and leadership. When we suggest a course of action, other people respond positively. Maybe we've invested substantial amounts of our time and money in gaining authority in the form of training and certificates and degrees. We look at Jesus and see authority—as early as age twelve in the temple engaging powerfully with the scribes; standing up in his hometown synagogue and boldly proclaiming himself the fulfillment of the prophet Isaiah's vision; confounding Pilate and the Jewish leaders even when he was arrested in chains; breathing on his disciples after his resurrection and giving them his Spirit, telling them they were now commissioned to go into the whole world with his authority. Whether we identify with authority or aspire to it, Jesus is there.

WHAT LOVE LONGS TO BE

A ninety-second video advertising the GoPro line of cameras illustrates how these two seemingly opposite traits fit together exactly right. First, a helicopter drops the skier Cody Townsend at the top of a seemingly impossible, nearly vertical crevasse between two rock walls at the top of a snow-covered mountain. Thanks to the GoPro head-mounted camera, we follow him off the edge, plunging down through the narrow canyon and out, safely, just barely, onto the gentler slopes below. It is terrifying. (One person who shared it online said that as he watched, he "tightened every orifice in sympathy.") The video is also mesmerizing and exhilarating.

What makes this video so compelling and compulsively shareable? It's the combination of authority and vulnerability—Townsend's complete command of the sport of skiing plus his willingness to stretch that competence to its absolute limit, to the point where there was the real possibility of loss.

A video that showed authority without vulnerability might be impressive, but it would ultimately be boring. A video that showed gratuitous risk-taking without commensurate authority might be good for a few laughs in the genre of "stupid human tricks," but it would not provoke astonishment, admiration, or awe. What we truly admire in human beings is not authority alone or vulnerability alone—we seek both together. When authority and vulnerability are combined, you find true flourishing.

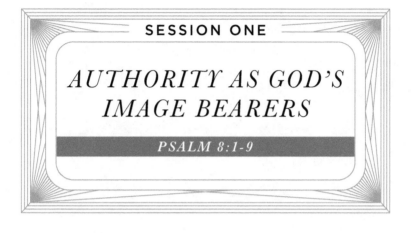

AUTHORITY AS GOD'S IMAGE BEARERS

PSALM 8:1-9

AUTHORITY IS *meant to characterize every image bearer.* This authority, uniquely ours as the image bearers of God, is a gift in every way. It does not come from our own autonomous selves—it is given by Another. And it is good.

Think of authority as *the capacity for meaningful action.* The first readers of the biblical command to "be fruitful and increase in number; fill the earth and subdue it" (Genesis 1:28) can only have had the faintest inkling of how human beings have been able to fulfill that call. The sorrow of the human story is not that we *have* authority; it is the way we have misused and neglected that authority.

SESSION GOAL	READ
Consider God's gift of trusting human beings with a measure of his authority.	Chapters 1 and 2 of *Strong and Weak*

REFLECT

❋ What are some ways our culture defines authority? Which of these seem godly? Which do not seem godly?

✳ How do you feel about being given authority (*the capacity
    for meaningful action*) by God?

≡≡⟫ **STUDY** ⟪≡≡

READ PSALM 8:1-9.

No other species has such a clear sense of responsibility for *other*
species—what Christian theology calls *dominion*, the capacity
and responsibility to act on behalf of the flourishing of the rest
of creation. The psalmist considered both the vastness of the
cosmos and the smallness of human beings in the midst of it,
then exclaimed his response in Psalm 8.

<blockquote>

¹ LORD, our Lord,

> how majestic is your name in all the earth!

You have set your glory

> in the heavens.

² Through the praise of children and infants

> you have established a stronghold against your enemies,
> to silence the foe and the avenger.

³ When I consider your heavens,

> the work of your fingers,

the moon and the stars,

> which you have set in place,

⁴ what is mankind that you are mindful of them,

> human beings that you care for them?

⁵ You have made them a little lower than the angels

> and crowned them with glory and honor.

</blockquote>

^{6} You made them rulers over the works of your hands;
>   you put everything under their feet:
^{7} all flocks and herds,
>   and the animals of the wild,
^{8} the birds in the sky,
>   and the fish in the sea,
>   all that swim the paths of the seas.
^{9} LORD, our Lord,
>   how majestic is your name in all the earth!

1. What authority does God give humans?

A common theme in the Hebrew Bible is weakness (that of children and infants) turned into strength. The work of God's fingers is vast, incomprehensible, and strong (v. 3), contrasting with the word in this psalm for the humans (v. 4), which is often associated with human frailty.[1]

2. If you were to read verses 2-4 aloud, what tone might you take? (Astonishment? wonder? surprise? incredulity?) If you're willing, say these verses aloud with that tone, or be curious about what tone naturally arises in your voice.

3. How are men and women crowned with glory and honor in a way that animals are not (v. 5; see also Genesis 1:27)?

> To put everything under human feet refers to the idea in Genesis 1:28 where dominion "does not indicate permission to exhaust the creation's resources but suggests that God grants to humans the honor of representing God in caring for all of creation."[2]

4. How do verses 5-8 resemble the creation account (Genesis 1:28; 2:19)?

5. The Psalmist opens and closes with the word *majestic*. If a child were to ask you what "majestic" means, what would you say?

> The envelope of the psalm (beginning and end) is about God, whereas the body of the text is about human dominion, making the psalm centered on God, not humans. Human dominion is a gift from God the Creator. The use of power without the praise of God would exploit creation and corrupt the psalm's hope.[3]

6. What does the fact that this psalm is centered on God and not humans tell us about how humans can best exercise any authority given to us?

Psalm 8 follows seven psalms full to the brim with enemies. Human suffering (Psalms 1–7) does not diminish the royal place and vocation of humanity to care for God's creation.

7. Why is it important for humans to know that authority (Psalm 8) exists for humans in spite of weakness and suffering (Psalms 1–7)?

RESPOND

☀ In what areas of life have you been given responsibility or the capacity for meaningful action (authority)?

✳ How does Psalm 8 shed light on that responsibility?

──≋ PRAY ≋──

As you pray this week, try paraphrasing Psalm 8 in light of a responsibility you bear in your life, even if it's as simple as caring for your home or car.

──≋ NEXT STEPS ≋──

This week as you water plants, do yardwork, or take care of pets, consider in wonder how God has given you the gift of dominion in caring for these creatures. If you do this work, try approaching it in the tone you found in question 2.

---

[1]Walter Brueggemann and William H. Bellinger Jr., *Psalms* (Cambridge: Cambridge University Press, 2014), 59.
[2]Brueggemann and Bellinger, *Psalms*, 59.
[3]Brueggemann and Bellinger, *Psalms*, 60-61.

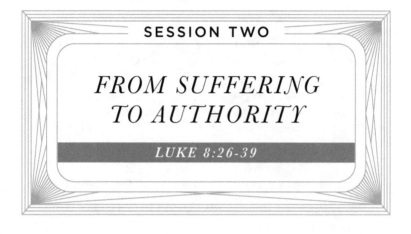

ABBY, AN ASIAN AMERICAN PHYSICIAN, told this story:

"When I was eight years old, my dad took me with him to use the copy machine at a convenience store. He was born in China, and his English was poor. He couldn't figure out how to get the copy machine to work, and couldn't explain his problem to the store owner. The owner mocked my dad's Chinese accent, ripped up his papers, and tossed them on the floor. Then he told us to get out of his store."

Abby paused. "I had always known my father as strong, kind, and smart. I had never seen him humiliated like that. He was so ashamed." That afternoon eight-year-old Abby discovered what it is like to live with vulnerability without authority.

Those of us with power have failed to address the persistent suffering of others. The consequences of our failure to fully bear the authoritative divine image fall most heavily on those who live in continual vulnerability. The only sustainable response is *to help build lasting authority* for those who do not have it.

SESSION GOAL	**READ**
To examine how bringing the power of the presence of Christ into messy situations can give authority to those who lack it.	Chapter 3 of *Strong and Weak*

⚞ REFLECT ⚟

✳ When has someone stood up for you? Or, if you can't remember such a time, when would you have liked someone to stand up for you?

✳ What qualities do we need to have if we're going to empower others to move forward as they would like?

⚞ STUDY ⚟

READ LUKE 8:26-39.

Jesus went out of his way to sail across the sea of Galilee to enter a messy personal and social situation. He used his power and presence to end a man's suffering and give him authority to share the goodness of God.

²⁶ They sailed to the region of the Gerasenes, which is across the lake from Galilee. ²⁷ When Jesus stepped ashore, he was met by a demon-possessed man from the town. For a long time this man had not worn clothes or lived in a house, but had lived in the tombs. ²⁸ When he saw Jesus, he cried out and fell at his feet, shouting at the top of his voice, "What do you want with me, Jesus, Son of the Most High God? I beg you, don't torture me!" ²⁹ For Jesus had commanded the impure spirit to come out of the man. Many times it had seized him, and though he was chained hand and foot and kept under guard, he had broken his chains and had been driven by the demon into solitary places.

³⁰ Jesus asked him, "What is your name?"

"Legion," he replied, because many demons had gone into him. ³¹ And they begged Jesus repeatedly not to order them to go into the Abyss.

³² A large herd of pigs was feeding there on the hillside. The demons begged Jesus to let them go into the pigs, and he gave them permission. ³³ When the demons came out of the man, they went into the pigs, and the herd rushed down the steep bank into the lake and was drowned.

³⁴ When those tending the pigs saw what had happened, they ran off and reported this in the town and countryside, ³⁵ and the people went out to see what had happened. When they came to Jesus, they found the man from whom the demons had gone out, sitting at Jesus' feet, dressed and in his right mind; and they were afraid. ³⁶ Those who had seen it told the people how the demon-possessed man had been cured. ³⁷ Then all the people of the region of the Gerasenes asked Jesus to leave them, because they were overcome with fear. So he got into the boat and left.

³⁸ The man from whom the demons had gone out begged to go with him, but Jesus sent him away, saying, ³⁹ "Return home and tell how much God has done for you." So the man went away and told all over town how much Jesus had done for him.

1. If you put yourself in the place of the disciples, what details about Legion's person and appearance would have been most alarming to you (vv. 26-29)?

2. How did Jesus show respect for the man possessed by demons—not treating him as if he were just one more needy person?

3. In what ways was this man vulnerable and suffering both before and after Jesus delivered him?

The stampede of the pigs would have created a dust cloud seen for miles and served as a testimony that the demons had truly left the man. This proof of freedom and cleansing from the demons was important for the townspeople to see so that they would accept the man back into society and not try to chain him up once again. In a sense, the pigs partnered with Jesus in creating a picture of the man's new freedom.

4. How did Jesus show respect for the healed man by making him a partner in his mission?

The man formerly called Legion was found "sitting at Jesus' feet," which was a way to say that he had become a disciple of Jesus (v. 35). Jesus must have spent some time teaching and interacting with the man. He then urged him to tell how much God had done for him (v. 39). The man seems to have done a good job, because when Jesus later returned to this region, people already knew who he was (Mark 6:54).[1]

5. Why might the people of the region of the Gerasenes have been afraid of Jesus rather than believing in him through the miraculous healing of the man?

> Some interpreters think the inhabitants of the region
> feared they would lose out economically if Jesus
> continued destroying swine. Others think they were
> afraid of the one who exercised such power. It was
> not the kind of reverent awe that Jesus could use
> constructively; it was a terror that repelled.[2]

6. How does having clarity about one's mission give people courage to take risks, to venture into messiness as Jesus did?

7. What do you think must have been true about Jesus' presence that made the man desire to go with Jesus (v. 38)?

RESPOND

* What helps us have the courage to help, defend, or stand up for someone who is suffering?

✳ What is a situation in the life of someone you know that you wish to ask Jesus to give you courage and authority to act in or speak into?

PRAY

Pray for someone you know who lives in vulnerability without authority. Ask God if there's something you need to do to be of assistance.

NEXT STEPS

This week, when you hesitate to step out, ask Jesus for a simple next step. Just one next step doesn't sound so overwhelming and will help you grow in authority.

---

[1]Jan Johnson, *Meeting God in Scripture* (Downers Grove, IL: InterVarsity Press, 2016), 55.
[2]Ray Summers, *Commentary on Luke* (Waco, TX: Word Books, 1972), 256.

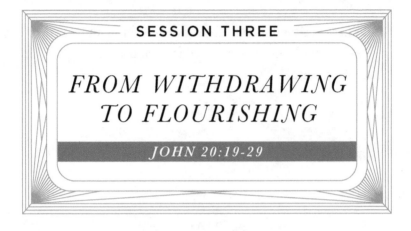

A CRUISE IS FINE AS A VACATION for a few days. But what if your whole life were a cruise? Year after year of others deciding where you will go and what's for dinner, anticipating your needs and protecting you from any real harm? That would feel less than human.

We are meant for more than leisure. This is true for our own sakes, but it is also true because we are still responsible to engage with the neighbors and the created order we have neglected, who have no option to board a cruise away from vulnerability. To disengage from the profound needs of those caught in suffering is to reject the call to bear the image of God.

The good news about escaping the Withdrawing quadrant is that any move—toward either authority or vulnerability—is a step in the right direction. Perhaps the two best beginning moves for those of us swaddled in affluence and intoxicated by our technology are into the natural world: the world of stars, snow and rain, trees and deserts—and into the relational world: the world of bodies with heartbeats, hands, and faces.

SESSION GOAL	**READ**
Explore the movement from withdrawal to the adventure of living with authority and vulnerability.	Chapter 4 of *Strong and Weak*

REFLECT

✳ What are some major reasons people prefer safety to engaging with people they don't know, or life situations that seem risky?

✳ What signs, if any, do you see in your life that you pull back from getting involved with people and situations that seem unusual to you?

STUDY

READ JOHN 20:19-29.

Thomas the disciple had good reasons to withdraw into safety. Nearly all the disciples disassociated from Jesus as he was declared a criminal and executed. Then the unthinkable happened. No one expected Jesus to come back from the dead. Messiahs were supposed to conquer oppressive nations, not death! In this passage, Jesus chose to draw Thomas back to himself by the authority of his appearance and the vulnerability of showing his wounds.

[19] On the evening of that first day of the week, when the disciples were together, with the doors locked for fear of the Jewish leaders, Jesus came and stood among them and said, "Peace be with you!" [20] After he said this, he showed them his hands and side. The disciples were overjoyed when they saw the Lord.

[21] Again Jesus said, "Peace be with you! As the Father has sent me, I am sending you." [22] And with that he breathed on them and said, "Receive the Holy Spirit. [23] If you forgive anyone's sins, their sins are forgiven; if you do not forgive them, they are not forgiven."

[24] Now Thomas (also known as Didymus), one of the Twelve, was not with the disciples when Jesus came. [25] So the other disciples told him, "We have seen the Lord!"

But he said to them, "Unless I see the nail marks in his hands and put my finger where the nails were, and put my hand into his side, I will not believe."

[26] A week later his disciples were in the house again, and Thomas was with them. Though the doors were locked, Jesus came and stood among them and said, "Peace be with you!" [27] Then he said to Thomas, "Put your finger here; see my hands. Reach out your hand and put it into my side. Stop doubting and believe."

[28] Thomas said to him, "My Lord and my God!"

[29] Then Jesus told him, "Because you have seen me, you have believed; blessed are those who have not seen and yet have believed."

1. Why were Jesus' words "peace be with you" such an appropriate greeting to offer the disciples at this time (v. 19)?

2. What accounts for the disciples being overjoyed at seeing Jesus, especially the wounds on his hands and side?

Notice that Jesus breathed on the disciples, telling them to receive the Holy Spirit, just as God "breathed into [Adam's] nostrils the breath of life, and the man became a living being" (Genesis 2:7). The disciples were familiar with the Torah and would have noticed this similarity of action.

3. What do the various greetings and commissions that Jesus gives the disciples seem to indicate or point toward (vv. 21-23)?

4. Why might Thomas have "played it safe" in not believing Jesus was truly alive, even to the point of disbelieving his fellow disciples (vv. 24-25)?

Thomas is "a muddled, dogged disciple, determined not to be taken in, standing on his rights not to believe anything until he's got solid evidence, confronted by a smiling Jesus who has just walked, as he did the previous week, through a locked door. 'My master,' Thomas says, 'and my God?' [Thomas] is the first person in [the book of John] to look at Jesus of Nazareth and address the word 'God' directly to him."[1]

5. What feelings did the previously doubtful, possibly baffled Thomas exhibit when he saw Jesus and they spoke to each other (vv. 26-28)?

What Jesus said in verse 29 "isn't so much a rebuke to Thomas; it's more of an encouragement to those who come later, to people of subsequent generations. We are all 'blessed' when, without having seen the risen Lord for ourselves, we nevertheless believe in him."[2]

6. How might people be encouraged today by Jesus' words, "blessed are those who have not seen and yet have believed"?

7. In what way are people today leaving safety behind and stepping into flourishing by believing in Jesus as their Lord and God, even though they have not seen him in bodily form?

> What we cannot see when we are caught in withdrawing is that there is something far better ahead, pleasures that we must be made strong enough to bear. We will only discover them if someone unbinds us and calls us forth. And the great glad news of the gospel is that someone has.

RESPOND

✳ When have you stepped out instead of "playing it safe" and found blessing?

✳ What might be God's invitation to you to move from playing it safe to flourishing—being fully alive, even participating in the glorious things God is doing today?

═══◄ PRAY ►═══

As you pray this week, ask that the Holy Spirit breathe into you the courage to participate with God more fully in what God is doing in your life and the lives of others.

═══◄ NEXT STEPS ►═══

As you move through the week, notice the times when you play it safe. In those moments, if possible, ask God what blessing might be waiting for you if you were to engage fully in the situation.

[1]N. T. Wright, *John for Everyone: Part Two* (London: SPCK, 2004), 152.
[2]Wright, *John for Everyone: Part Two*, 153, 154.

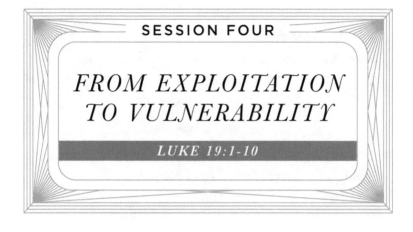

FROM EXPLOITATION TO VULNERABILITY

LUKE 19:1-10

FLOURISHING REQUIRES both authority *and* vulnerability in equal measure. But we usually do not pursue these two good things with the same wholeheartedness. Most of us move more toward authority and control than toward vulnerability. Why? Authority involves possible gain while vulnerability involves possible loss.

As we move toward authority, we turn to habits, substances, or patterns of thought (entertainment, alcohol, coffee, blaming) as props when we feel vulnerable. These things seem to offer *control*, for the essence of control is authority without vulnerability, acting without any possibility of loss. But control is an illusion. Our props inevitably fail us, which causes us to grasp more intensely for the control we thought they promised.

The best early warning sign that you are drifting toward craving authority and exploitation is that your closest relationships—which demand the greatest personal risk for you—begin to decay. Those who depend on you for love, friendship, and support sink into increased vulnerability, even perhaps suffering. Worst off are those already at risk—the youngest, the oldest, those who contribute the least to our sensations of power. They can flourish only if we resist the temptations of exploiting.

SESSION GOAL	READ
Observe how exploitation is not a gain but a loss, defeating any sense of flourishing.	Chapter 5 of *Strong and Weak*

⎯⎯⎯ REFLECT ⎯⎯⎯

❋ How does the desire to control people and situations diminish the energy and spirit of life?

❋ Where do you find yourself trying to protect yourself against loss?

⎯⎯⎯ STUDY ⎯⎯⎯

READ LUKE 19:1-10.

Tax collector was a powerful but despised role. In this passage, Zacchaeus limited his power, entering the precarious circumstances of mixing in a crowd, eventually repaying and even giving away the money that had brought him such privilege and power.

> ¹ Jesus entered Jericho and was passing through. ² A man was there by the name of Zacchaeus; he was a chief tax collector and was wealthy. ³ He wanted to see who Jesus

was, but because he was short he could not see over the crowd. ⁴ So he ran ahead and climbed a sycamore-fig tree to see him, since Jesus was coming that way.

⁵ When Jesus reached the spot, he looked up and said to him, "Zacchaeus, come down immediately. I must stay at your house today." ⁶ So he came down at once and welcomed him gladly.

⁷ All the people saw this and began to mutter, "He has gone to be the guest of a sinner."

⁸ But Zacchaeus stood up and said to the Lord, "Look, Lord! Here and now I give half of my possessions to the poor, and if I have cheated anybody out of anything, I will pay back four times the amount."

⁹ Jesus said to him, "Today salvation has come to this house, because this man, too, is a son of Abraham. ¹⁰ For the Son of Man came to seek and to save the lost."

Chief tax collectors skimmed money off the income of other tax collectors who skimmed money off Jewish citizens. These people were hated and considered unclean. Lying to them was condoned.¹

1. What kind of life did someone like Zacchaeus (who had publicly cheated many people) lead?

It's likely that Zacchaeus needed to climb the tree not just because he was short, but also because it wouldn't have been safe for him to walk unprotected in a crowd. Adult males would not have shamed themselves by climbing a tree, but perhaps Zacchaeus thought the leafy sycamore would shield him from harm and from view.[2]

2. Why do you think a known extortionist (as tax collectors were) would want to see Jesus and welcome him gladly into his home? (Consider also Luke 15:1-2.)

3. If you had been in the crowd, what might you have expected a rabbi to say to Zacchaeus?

4. Why do you think Jesus changed his plans from just passing through Jericho to get to Jerusalem to inviting himself to spend the day and night with Zacchaeus (vv. 1, 5)?

5. How might the disciples have responded to this change of plans?

> Jesus' request that Zacchaeus provide lodging would have been a "demonstration of costly love. After receiving such love, Zacchaeus will never be the same. This account presents a rare view of a person who has received costly love from Jesus, and it records his response."[3]

6. How might choosing to visit Zacchaeus have affected people's opinion of Jesus, which was already on the verge of turning on him as he approached Jerusalem this last time (v. 7)?

> Jewish law required restitution of the principal amount and a fifth more (Numbers 5:7), while Zacchaeus promised four times what he had extorted.

7. In what way did Jesus affirm that Zacchaeus was entering a flourishing life even though he promised to give away (lose) what he had wrongfully gained (v. 9)?

᠅᠁᠅ RESPOND ᠅᠁᠅

✳ Where have you feared loss in the past but now might want to show confidence in God's provision?

✳ How might God be leading you to come alongside someone who has been taken advantage of and restore their respect and even resources?

᠅᠁᠅ PRAY ᠅᠁᠅

Ask God for opportunities to come alongside someone who has been taken advantage of and to help restore their dignity.

᠅᠁᠅ NEXT STEPS ᠅᠁᠅

Try to notice people around you who have true spiritual authority (but perhaps not positions of expertise) as well as equal amounts of vulnerability. If you're willing, ask them what helps them with this.

[1]Kenneth E. Bailey, *Jesus Through Middle Eastern Eyes: Cultural Studies in the Gospels* (Downers Grove, IL: InterVarsity Press, 2008), 177.

[2]Jan Johnson, "From Gangster to Giver," in *Meeting God in Scripture* (Downers Grove, IL: InterVarsity Press, 2016), 106.

[3]Bailey, *Jesus Through Middle Eastern Eyes*, 181.

A DIFFERENT KIND
OF VULNERABILITY

What I mean by *vulnerability* is a bit different from its standard usage in the United States today, where it is often limited to personal and emotional transparency. We see this when celebrities and ordinary people disclose all kinds of seemingly shameful or incriminating details about their lives.

The vulnerability that leads to flourishing requires *exposure to meaningful risk*, which is the possibility of loss—the chance that when we act, we will lose something we value. To risk is to open ourselves up to the chance that something will go wrong, that something will be taken from us—without knowing for sure whether that loss will come to pass or not.

To be vulnerable is to be exposed to the possibility of loss—and not just loss of things or possessions, but loss of our own sense of self. *Vulnerable* at root means *woundable.* Wounded, we are forced to become careful, tender, tentative in the way we move in the world, if we can still move on our own at all. To be vulnerable is to open oneself up to the possibility that the result of our action in the world will be a wound or something lost, potentially never to be gained again.

We are not talking about risking things we don't care whether we keep or lose, playing poker with chips that never have to be cashed in. True vulnerability involves risking something of real and even irreplaceable value.

I have come to believe that the image of God is not just evident in our authority over creation—it is also evident in our vulnerability in the midst of creation.

Psalm 8 speaks of authority and vulnerability in the same breath because this is what it means to bear the image of God.

When the true image bearer came, the "image of the invisible God" (Colossians 1:15), he came with unparalleled authority. Jesus had more capacity for meaningful action than any other person who has lived. His actions all took their place within the story of Israel, the greatest of all shared histories, and these actions decisively changed the path of history and created a new and different shared future.

And yet Jesus, too, was born naked like us, as dependent and therefore vulnerable as any human being. And though the Western artistic tradition has placed loincloths over the uncomfortable truth of crucifixion, he died naked as well. He died exposed to the possibility of loss, not just of his human life but of his very identity as the divine Son with whom the Father was well pleased. He was laid in the dust of death, the final and full expression of loss. And in all of this, he was not just Very Man but Very God. (Adapted from *Strong and Weak*, 40-46)

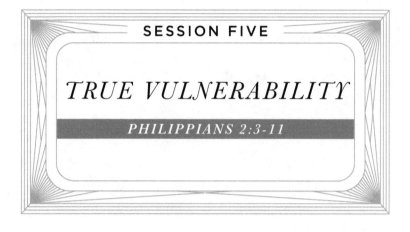

TRUE VULNERABILITY

PHILIPPIANS 2:3-11

BEFORE WE CAN MOVE into greater authority and greater vulnerability, we first have to take the journey to *hidden vulnerability* —the willingness to bear burdens and expose ourselves to risks that others cannot fully see or understand. This may take the form of the leader's own personal exposures to risk that often remain unspoken, unseen, and unimagined by others. Jesus experienced this.

The second journey we must take is *descending to the dead*, which is the choice to visit the most broken corners of the world and of our own heart. We become willing to actively embrace suffering. Our mission in the world is to help individuals and communities to be set free from addiction, injustice, and tyranny. To do so, we must do what no one wants to do: voluntarily expose ourselves to pain and loss. Jesus did this as well.

Only after we have made these journeys will we be the kind of people who can be entrusted with true power, the power that rescues others who have been trapped in tyranny, apathy, and poverty.

SESSION GOAL	**READ**
Consider how Christ gave himself up to suffering and walking with people through pain and loss.	Chapters 6 and 7 of *Strong and Weak*

REFLECT

* When, if ever, have you seen someone give up something that could have been used to their own advantage? (For example, money, possessions, or even credit for a task done well.) What were the risks involved?

* How are people affected by walking with others through pain and loss? Have you experienced this?

STUDY

READ PHILIPPIANS 2:3-11.

This passage describes humility and vulnerability and then presents, in what is thought to be an early Christian hymn, how Jesus lived this out in both his humanity and deity.

³ Do nothing out of selfish ambition or vain conceit. Rather, in humility value others above yourselves, ⁴ not

looking to your own interests but each of you to the interests of the others.

⁵ In your relationships with one another, have the same mindset as Christ Jesus:

⁶ Who, being in very nature God,
  did not consider equality with God something to be
   used to his own advantage;
⁷ rather, he made himself nothing
  by taking the very nature of a servant,
  being made in human likeness.
⁸ And being found in appearance as a man,
  he humbled himself
  by becoming obedient to death—
   even death on a cross!
⁹ Therefore God exalted him to the highest place
  and gave him the name that is above every name,
¹⁰ that at the name of Jesus every knee should bow,
  in heaven and on earth and under the earth,
¹¹ and every tongue acknowledge that Jesus Christ is
  Lord,
  to the glory of God the Father.

1. How was Jesus' mind set on looking to the interests of others, not his own?

> "Value others above yourselves" may sound self-
> demeaning and codependent—but consider how
> that approach counters our automatic tendencies
> to think we're right or that we know more than
> others. By aiming high—to treat others as *better* than
> ourselves—we may at least value others as we value
> ourselves, even treat them with respect and dignity.

2. Why is it helpful and wise to look to the interests of others, keeping in mind that *agape* love is wanting what is best for others?

> Jesus didn't stop being divine; he retained his equality
> with God. The point of the cross is that "Jesus didn't
> regard this equality as something to take advantage
> of, something to exploit. . . . The incarnate Son
> of God dying on the cross is the true meaning of
> who God is. He is the God of self-giving love."[1]

3. What limitations did Jesus take upon himself by living as a human?

4. In what way was Jesus obedient to death (v. 8)?

5. How does giving Jesus "the highest place" in our life and in all reality affect our relationships with others?

6. What creatures "in heaven and on earth and under the earth" might Paul be referring to when he says that all will bow before Jesus?

Jesus was vulnerable, yet never a victim. He could have stopped the entire process—trial, torture, crucifixion— at any time. But he was clear about his goals. "Do you think I cannot call on my Father, and he will at once put at my disposal more than twelve legions of angels? But how then would the Scriptures be fulfilled that say it must happen in this way?" (Matthew 26:53-54).

7. What do the phrases "equality with God" and "the name that is above every other name" suggest about relations within Trinity?

> Within the Trinity there is "not even a thought of 'First, Second, and Third.' There is no subordination within the Trinity, not because of some profound metaphysical fact, but because the members of the Trinity will not have it."[2]

⚛ RESPOND ⚛

✳ What might God be inviting you to risk or to give up?

✳ How does the suffering vulnerability of Jesus help us today as we suffer?

⚛ PRAY ⚛

Ask God to help you embrace the sacrifice of Jesus in such a way that you are gladly vulnerable in helping others move ahead.

━━━▧ NEXT STEPS ▨━━━

Consider how firefighters show strength by making themselves vulnerable and perhaps even available to be sacrificed to ensure the safety of others. As you move through this week, ask God to give you strength to make yourself vulnerable for the sake of others, even in the smallest ways.

Study the account of Jesus' transfiguration in Luke 9:28-36. Then reread the discussion of this passage in *Strong and Weak* chapter six. Reflect on any insights you gain related to your current roles and sense of calling.

---

[1]Tom Wright, *Paul for Everyone: The Prison Letters—Ephesians, Philippians, Colossians, and Philemon* (London: SPCK, 2002), 102-3.

[2]Dallas Willard, *Renovation of the Heart: Putting On the Character of Christ* (Colorado Springs, CO: NavPress, 2002), 184.

FIRMNESS AND WARMTH

EPHESIANS 4:11-16, 25-29

IN FLOURISHING RELATIONSHIPS, authority exerts itself as firmness while vulnerability exhibits itself as warmth. We tend to lean one way or the other because we see firmness and warmth as opposites. But they are not; they can go together. In fact, they must go together.

For example, in parenting, firmness without warmth (authoritarian parenting) leads eventually to rebellion. Warmth without firmness (indulgent parenting) leads eventually to spoiled, entitled brats. *Either one* without the other creates a poor environment in which children will not flourish.

To be firm and warm results in kindness (quadrant I). But kindness and warmth are not the same as being "nice." Niceness drifts down to the bottom right (quadrant II), settling for easy, warm feelings without ever setting appropriate boundaries. Kindness, on the other hand, manages to be clear and firm while also tender and affectionate. Much of the dysfunction of our lives comes from oscillating along the line of false choice, never seeing that embracing both firmness and warmth helps us learn to be kind, flourishing people.

SESSION GOAL	**READ**
Explore how authority and vulnerability in relationships are expressed as firmness and warmth.	Chapter 8 of *Strong and Weak*

REFLECT

✳ Would your friends say that you lean more toward firmness or warmth? Why might that be?

✳ When have you seen someone speak truth—perhaps a difficult truth—with great love?

STUDY

READ EPHESIANS 4:11-16, 25-29.

Maturity in Christ involves wisdom in discerning what is true, good, and beautiful. But truth loses its fullness when it is expressed without love. Truth and love as well as justice and mercy always travel together and must not be separated.

[11] So Christ himself gave the apostles, the prophets, the evangelists, the pastors and teachers, [12] to equip his people

for works of service, so that the body of Christ may be built up [13] until we all reach unity in the faith and in the knowledge of the Son of God and become mature, attaining to the whole measure of the fullness of Christ.

[14] Then we will no longer be infants, tossed back and forth by the waves, and blown here and there by every wind of teaching and by the cunning and craftiness of people in their deceitful scheming. [15] Instead, speaking the truth in love, we will grow to become in every respect the mature body of him who is the head, that is, Christ. [16] From him the whole body, joined and held together by every supporting ligament, grows and builds itself up in love, as each part does its work. . . .

[25] Therefore each of you must put off falsehood and speak truthfully to your neighbor, for we are all members of one body. [26] "In your anger do not sin": Do not let the sun go down while you are still angry, [27] and do not give the devil a foothold. [28] Anyone who has been stealing must steal no longer, but must work, doing something useful with their own hands, that they may have something to share with those in need.

[29] Do not let any unwholesome talk come out of your mouths, but only what is helpful for building others up according to their needs, that it may benefit those who listen.

1. What words in this passage reflect a life that is flourishing—fully alive, connected to our human purpose and to the heights and depths of divine glory?

2. What words in this passage are connected to authority and firmness—or lack of it?

3. What words in this passage are connected to vulnerability, kindness, and love?

4. What happens when someone speaks the truth with harshness or self-righteousness? When have you seen that happen?

5. How is avoiding the truth in an effort to be nice actually indulgent? When have you seen that happen?

There is a natural connection between justice and love. "Justice without love will *always* fall short of what needs to be done. . . . Justice without love will never do justice to justice, nor will 'love' without justice ever do justice to love. Indeed, it will not be love at all; *for love wills the good of what is loved*, and that must include justice where justice is lacking."[1]

6. How does the idea that love is willing what is best for another equip us to have the courage to speak the truth in love?

The great author Samuel Johnson was a devout Christian. "Despite the tendency of many of his friends to turn their conversation into displays of verbal brilliance, or into gossip and slander, he . . . was without malice." When asked what was the point of conversation in which "nobody said anything worth remembering," Johnson "replied that the point was 'to eat and drink together, and to promote kindness.'"[2]

7. In what ways do both authority and vulnerability "promote kindness"?

—────▧ **RESPOND** ▨───—

✳ In what situations would you like to be able to combine firmness with great warmth?

✳ When you are tempted to exclude either warmth or firmness in a relationship, what helps you get a right heart toward the other person?

—────▧ **PRAY** ▨───—

As you pray, thank God for his firm authority in creating justice, and the warm vulnerability of love. Ask God to help you embrace more fully both firmness and warmth to practically express love—willing what is best for others.

—────▧ **NEXT STEPS** ▨───—

This week, notice your tendency toward firmness or warmth and ask God for a measure of energy to embrace the other. As this happens, talk with God about what you learned about yourself and about relationships.

---

[1]Dallas Willard, *Knowing Christ Today* (New York: HarperOne, 2009), 80.
[2]Tom Wright, *Paul for Everyone: The Prison Letters—Ephesians, Philippians, Colossians, and Philemon* (London: SPCK, 2002), 54.

LEADING A
SMALL GROUP

LEADING A BIBLE DISCUSSION can be an enjoyable and rewarding experience. But it can also be intimidating—especially if you've never done it before. If this is how you feel, you're in good company.

Remember when God asked Moses to lead the Israelites out of Egypt? Moses replied, "Please send someone else" (Exodus 4:13)! But God gave Moses the help (human and divine) he needed to be a strong leader.

Leading a Bible discussion is not difficult if you follow certain guidelines. You don't need to be an expert on the Bible or a trained teacher. The suggestions listed below can help you to effectively fulfill your role as leader—and enjoy doing it.

PREPARING FOR THE STUDY

1. As you study the passage before the group meeting, ask God to help you understand it and apply it in your own life. Unless this happens, you will not be prepared to lead others. Pray too for the various members of the group. Ask God to open your hearts to the message of his Word and motivate you to action.

2. Read the introduction to the entire guide to get an overview of the subject at hand and the issues that will be explored.

3. Be ready to respond to the "Reflect" questions with a personal story or example. The group will be only as vulnerable and open as its leader.

4. Read the chapters of the companion book that are recommended at the beginning of the session.

5. Read and reread the assigned Bible passage to familiarize yourself with it. You may want to look up the passage in a Bible so that you can see its context.

6. This study guide is based on the New International Version of the Bible. It will help you and the group if you use this translation as the basis for your study and discussion.

7. Carefully work through each question in the study. Spend time in meditation and reflection as you consider how to respond.

8. Write your thoughts and responses in the space provided in the study guide. This will help you to express your understanding of the passage clearly.

9. It might help you to have a Bible dictionary handy. Use it to look up any unfamiliar words, names, or places.

10. Take the final (application) study questions and the "Respond" portion of each study seriously. Consider what this means for your life, what changes you may need to make in your lifestyle, or what actions you can take in your church or with people you know. Remember that the group will follow your lead in responding to the studies.

LEADING THE STUDY

1. Be sure everyone in your group has a study guide and a Bible. Encourage the group to prepare beforehand for each discussion by reading the introduction to the guide and by working through the questions for that session.

2. At the beginning of your first time together, explain that these studies are meant to be discussions, not lectures. Encourage the members of the group to participate. However, do not put pressure on those who may be hesitant to speak during the first few sessions.

3. Begin the study on time. Open with prayer, asking God to help the group understand and apply the passage.

4. Have a group member read aloud the introductory paragraphs at the beginning of the discussion. This will remind the group of the topic of the study.

5. Discuss the "Reflect" questions before reading the Bible passage. These kinds of opening questions are important for several reasons. First, there is usually a stiffness that needs to be overcome before people will begin to talk openly. A good question will break the ice.

   Second, most people will have lots of different things going on in their minds (dinner, an exam, an important meeting coming up, how to get the car fixed), which have nothing to do with the study. A creative question will get their attention and draw them into the discussion.

   Third, opening questions can reveal where our thoughts or feelings need to be transformed by Scripture. That is why it is important not to read the passage before the "Reflect" questions are asked. The passage will tend to color the honest reactions people would otherwise give, because they feel they are supposed to think the way the Bible does.

6. Have a group member read aloud the Scripture passage.

7. As you ask the questions, keep in mind that they are designed to be used just as they are written. You may simply read them aloud. Or you may prefer to express them in your own words.

There may be times when it is appropriate to deviate from the study guide. For example, a question may already have been answered. If so, move on to the next question. Or someone may raise an important question not covered in the guide. Take time to discuss it, but try to keep the group from going off on tangents.

8. Avoid offering the first answer to a study question. Repeat or rephrase questions if necessary until they are clearly understood. An eager group quickly becomes passive and silent if members think the leader will give all the *right* answers.

9. Don't be afraid of silence. People may need time to think about the question before formulating their answers.

10. Don't be content with just one answer. Ask, "What do the rest of you think?" or, "Anything else?" until several people have given answers to a question. You might point out one of the study sidebars to help spur discussion; for example, "Does the quotation on page seventeen provide any insight as you think about this question?"

11. Acknowledge all contributions. Be affirming whenever possible. Never reject an answer. If it is clearly off base, ask, "Which verse led you to that conclusion?" or, "What do the rest of you think?"

12. Don't expect every answer to be addressed to you, even though this will probably happen at first. As group members become more at ease, they will begin to truly interact with each other. This is one sign of healthy discussion.

13. Don't be afraid of controversy. It can be stimulating! If you don't resolve an issue completely, don't be frustrated. Move on and keep it in mind for later. A subsequent study may solve the problem.

14. Try to periodically summarize what the group has said about the passage. This helps to draw together the various ideas mentioned and gives continuity to the study. But don't preach.

15. When you come to the application questions at the end of each "Study" section, be willing to keep the discussion going by describing how you have been affected by the study. It's important that we each apply the message of the passage to ourselves in a specific way.

    Depending on the makeup of your group and the length of time you've been together, you may or may not want to discuss the "Respond" section. If not, allow the group to read it and reflect on it silently. Encourage members to make specific commitments and to write them in their study guide. Ask them the following week how they did with their commitments.

16. Conclude your time together with conversational prayer. Ask for God's help in following through on the commitments you've made.

17. End the group discussion on time.

Many more suggestions and helps are found in The Big Book on Small Groups *by Jeffrey Arnold.*

RECOMMENDED RESOURCES

Boundaries: When to Say Yes,
How to Say No to Take Control of Your Life
updated and expanded edition
Henry Cloud and John Townsend

Crucial Conversations
Kerry Patterson, Joseph Grenny,
Ron McMillan, and Al Switzler

A Force More Powerful documentary series
International Center on Nonviolent Conflict

Living a Purpose-Full Life:
What Happens When You Say Yes to God
Jan Johnson

Playing God: Redeeming the Gift of Power
Andy Crouch

Speaking the Truth in Love: How to Be an Assertive Christian
Ruth Koch and Kenneth C. Haugk

THE IVP SIGNATURE COLLECTION

Since 1947 InterVarsity Press has been publishing thoughtful Christian books that serve the university, the church, and the world. In celebration of our seventy-fifth anniversary, IVP is releasing special editions of select iconic and bestselling books from throughout our history.

RELEASED IN 2019

Basic Christianity (1958)
JOHN STOTT

How to Give Away Your Faith (1966)
PAUL E. LITTLE

RELEASED IN 2020

The God Who Is There (1968)
FRANCIS A. SCHAEFFER

This Morning with God (1968)
EDITED BY CAROL ADENEY AND BILL WEIMER

The Fight (1976)
JOHN WHITE

Free at Last? (1983)
CARL F. ELLIS JR.

The Dust of Death (1973)
OS GUINNESS

The Singer (1975)
CALVIN MILLER

RELEASED IN 2021

Knowing God (1973)
J. I. PACKER

Out of the Saltshaker and Into the World
(1979) REBECCA MANLEY PIPPERT

A Long Obedience in the Same Direction
(1980) EUGENE H. PETERSON

More Than Equals (1993)
SPENCER PERKINS AND CHRIS RICE

Between Heaven and Hell (1982)
PETER KREEFT

Good News About Injustice (1999)
GARY A. HAUGEN

The Challenge of Jesus (1999)
N. T. WRIGHT

Hearing God (1999)
DALLAS WILLARD

RELEASED IN 2022

The Heart of Racial Justice (2004)
BRENDA SALTER McNEIL AND
RICK RICHARDSON

Sacred Rhythms (2006)
RUTH HALEY BARTON

Habits of the Mind (2000)
JAMES W. SIRE

True Story (2008)
JAMES CHOUNG

Scribbling in the Sand (2002)
MICHAEL CARD

The Next Worship (2015)
SANDRA MARIA VAN OPSTAL

Delighting in the Trinity (2012)
MICHAEL REEVES

Strong and Weak (2016)
ANDY CROUCH

Liturgy of the Ordinary (2016)
TISH HARRISON WARREN

IVP SIGNATURE BIBLE STUDIES

As companions to the IVP Signature Collection, IVP Signature Bible Studies feature the inductive study method, equipping individuals and groups to explore the biblical truths embedded in these books.

Basic Christianity Bible Study
JOHN STOTT

How to Give Away Your Faith Bible Study
PAUL E. LITTLE

The Singer Bible Study, CALVIN MILLER

Knowing God Bible Study, J. I. PACKER

A Long Obedience in the Same Direction Bible Study, EUGENE H. PETERSON

Good News About Injustice Bible Study
GARY A. HAUGEN

Hearing God Bible Study
DALLAS WILLARD

The Heart of Racial Justice Bible Study
BRENDA SALTER McNEIL AND
RICK RICHARDSON

True Story Bible Study, JAMES CHOUNG

The Next Worship Bible Study
SANDRA MARIA VAN OPSTAL

Strong and Weak Bible Study
ANDY CROUCH